US WE ME + YOU

LARKINROAD

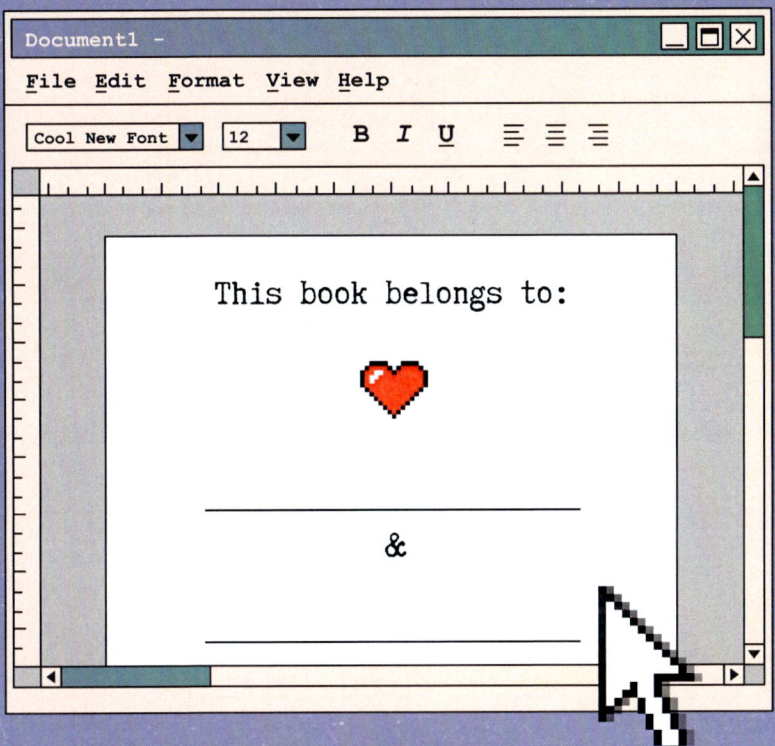

Document1 -

File Edit Format View Help

Cool New Font ▼ 12 ▼ **B** *I* U̲ ≡ ≡ ≡

This book belongs to:

_____

&

_____

me & you

How it works

There are no right or wrong answers with this book!

This is a journal for two partners:

♥ Partner 1 fills out pages marked #1

♥ Partner 2 fills out pages marked #2

♥ Play each game and answer each question honestly and openly

♥ Laughing is ENCOURAGED!

♥ Take your time answering & compare answers at the end!

FIRSTS:

What did our first text say?

Where did we first meet?

Where was our first date?

Who kissed who first?

Who said I love you first?

When did we first meet each others family?

First movie we saw together?

#1

FIRSTS:

What did our first text say?

Where did we first meet?

Where was our first date?

Who kissed who first?

Who said I love you first?

When did we first meet each others family?

First movie we saw together?

#2

what was your

F I R S T

impression of

M E ?

what was your

FIRST

impression of

ME?

WHAT IS OUR

FAVORITE PLACE

WE'VE EVER GONE TOGETHER?

WHAT IS OUR

FAVORITE PLACE

WE'VE EVER GONE TOGETHER?

Top Three Dates

WE'VE EVER BEEN ON:

1. _____

2. _____

3. _____

WHAT DO YOU THINK YOUR PARTNER SAID FOR THEIR #1 DATE?

1. _____

Top Three Dates

WE'VE EVER BEEN ON:

1. _____

2. _____

3. _____

WHAT DO YOU THINK YOUR PARTNER SAID FOR THEIR #1 DATE?

1. _____

IF WE COULD HAVE *dinner* WITH ANYONE LIVING OR DEAD, *who would it be?*

IF WE COULD HAVE

dinner

WITH ANYONE

LIVING

OR DEAD,

*who would
it be?*

OUR FAVORITES:

MOVIE GENRE:

DATE SPOT:

SNACK:

HOBBY:

ICE CREAM SPOT:

GAME:

RESTAURANT:

OUTDOOR ACTIVITY:

COFFEE SHOP:

1

OUR FAVORITES:

MOVIE GENRE:

DATE SPOT:

SNACK:

HOBBY:

ICE CREAM SPOT:

GAME:

RESTAURANT:

OUTDOOR ACTIVITY:

COFFEE SHOP:

2

A ♥ one word to describe yourself: ♥

A ♥ one word to describe your partner: ♥

#1

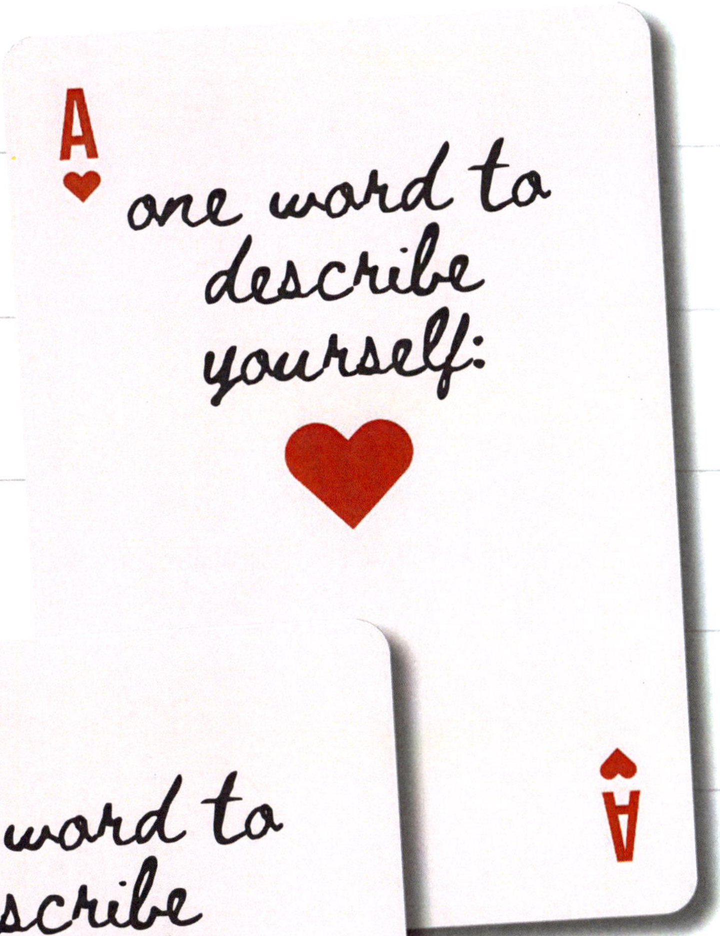

A ♥ one word to
describe
yourself:

♥

A ♥

A ♥ one word to
describe
your partner:

♥

A ♥

#2

RELATIONSHIP SUPERLATIVES

MOST LIKELY TO

**BINGE WATCH
A SHOW IN ONE SITTING**

**GET LOST,
EVEN WITH GPS**

**FALL ASLEEP
FIRST**

**GET
HANGRY**

**OVERSHARE
WITH STRANGERS**

**ORDER
DESSERT FIRST**

**CRY DURING
A MOVIE**

**TAKE A MILLION
PHOTOS ON VACA**

#1

MOST LIKELY TO

BINGE WATCH
A SHOW IN ONE SITTING

GET LOST,
EVEN WITH GPS

FALL ASLEEP
FIRST

GET
HANGRY

OVERSHARE
WITH STRANGERS

ORDER
DESSERT FIRST

CRY DURING
A MOVIE

TAKE A MILLION
PHOTOS ON VACA

#2

if we could only eat

one dessert together for the rest of our lives,

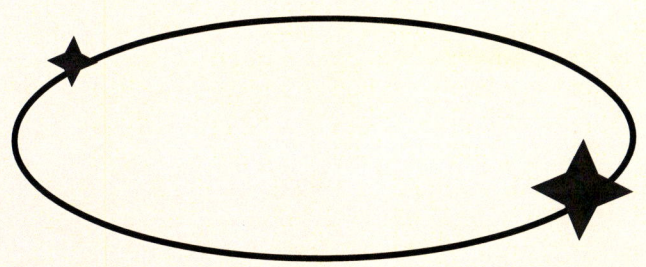

what would it be?

#1

if we could only eat

one dessert together for the rest of our lives,

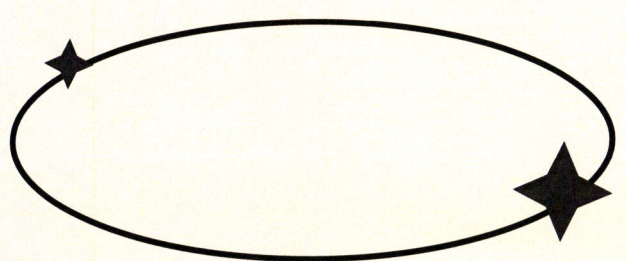

what would it be?

#2

FREAKY FRIDAY

If we switched bodies for a day:

**How would you spend a free afternoon
if you had my hobbies?**

**What would you wear if you had to
dress like me for a day?**

**What would you like most
about my daily schedule?**

FREAKY FRIDAY

If we switched bodies for a day:

**How would you spend a free afternoon
if you had my hobbies?**

**What would you wear if you had to
dress like me for a day?**

**What would you like most
about my daily schedule?**

WHAT IS SOMETHING
PEOPLE MIGHT BE

SURPRISED

TO
KNOW

ABOUT US?

#1

WHAT IS SOMETHING
PEOPLE MIGHT BE

SURPRISED

TO
KNOW

ABOUT US?

#2

if we won the lottery...

what's the first thing we would do?

if we won the lottery...
what's the first thing we would do?

WOULD YOU RATHER

COFFEE	TEA
SALTY	SWEET
MOUNTAINS	BEACH
MORNING PERSON	NIGHT OWL
EAT AT HOME	GO TO RESTAURANT
CHOCOLATE	VANILLA

WOULD YOUR PARTNER RATHER

COFFEE	TEA
SALTY	SWEET
MOUNTAINS	BEACH
MORNING PERSON	NIGHT OWL
EAT AT HOME	GO TO RESTAURANT
CHOCOLATE	VANILLA

WOULD YOU RATHER

COFFEE	TEA
SALTY	SWEET
MOUNTAINS	BEACH
MORNING PERSON	NIGHT OWL
EAT AT HOME	GO TO RESTAURANT
CHOCOLATE	VANILLA

WOULD YOUR PARTNER RATHER

COFFEE	TEA
SALTY	SWEET
MOUNTAINS	BEACH
MORNING PERSON	NIGHT OWL
EAT AT HOME	GO TO RESTAURANT
CHOCOLATE	VANILLA

WHAT IS YOUR

Favorite
Memory

OF US?

#1

WHAT IS YOUR

Favorite
Memory

OF US?

1

WHAT IS SOMETHING THAT WE'VE

LEARNED

THE HARD

WAY

IN OUR RELATIONSHIP?

WHAT IS SOMETHING THAT WE'VE

LEARNED THE HARD WAY

IN OUR RELATIONSHIP?

WOULD YOU RATHER

CIRCLE ONE:

only be able to

whisper
or
shout
to each other

have your search
history sent to

your boss
or
your partner's
parents

be able to

read each
others minds
or
see the
future

have a

personal
chef
or
daily
cleaning service

WOULD YOU RATHER

CIRCLE ONE:

only be able to

whisper

or

shout
to each other

have your search
history sent to

your boss

or

your partner's
parents

be able to

read each
others minds

or

see the
future

have a
personal
chef

or

daily
cleaning service

WHAT IS OUR SONG?
WHAT IS A SONG
THAT REPRESENTS
OUR RELATIONSHIP?

#1

WHAT IS OUR SONG?
WHAT IS A SONG
THAT REPRESENTS
OUR RELATIONSHIP?

#2

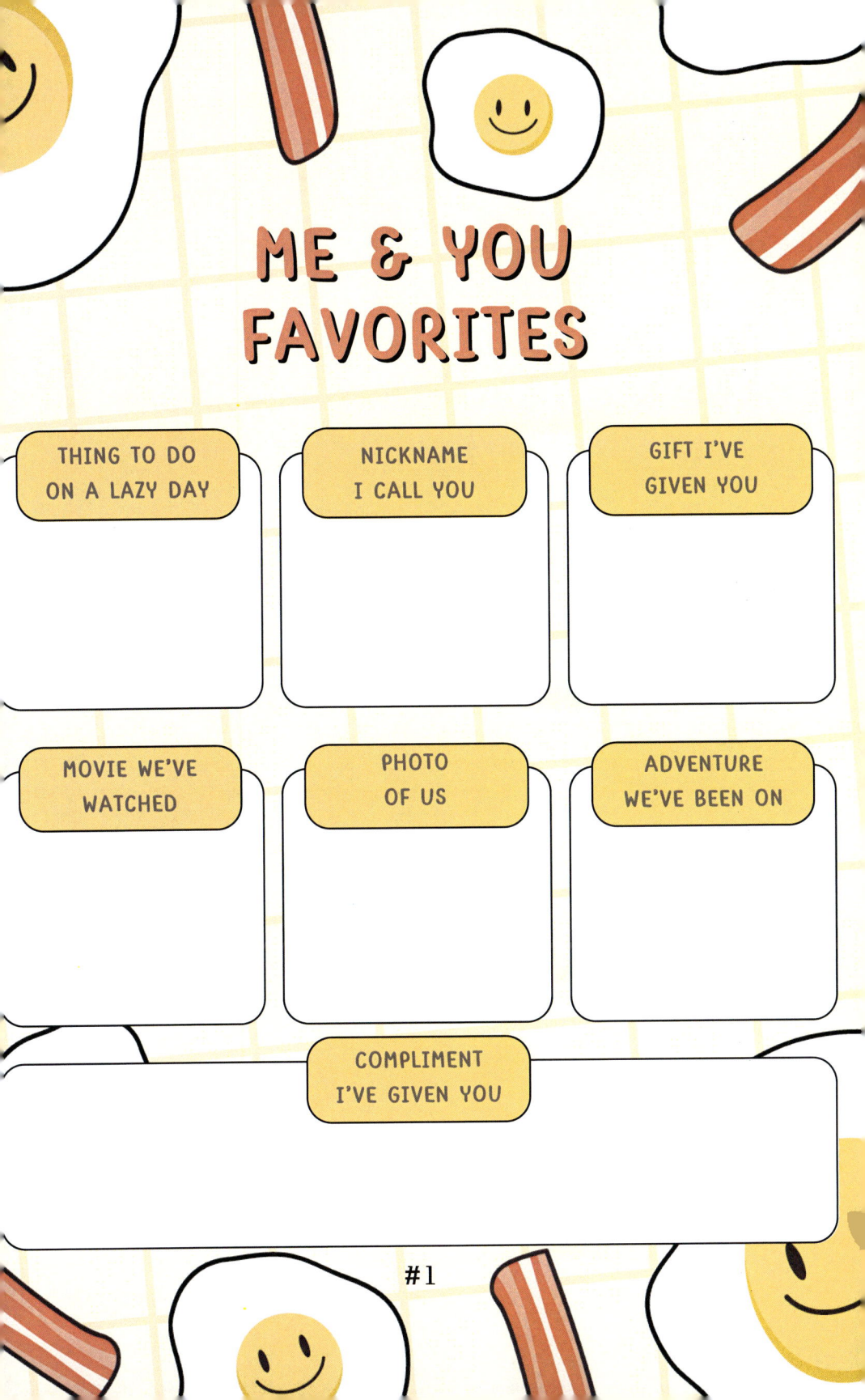

ME & YOU FAVORITES

THING TO DO ON A LAZY DAY

NICKNAME I CALL YOU

GIFT I'VE GIVEN YOU

MOVIE WE'VE WATCHED

PHOTO OF US

ADVENTURE WE'VE BEEN ON

COMPLIMENT I'VE GIVEN YOU

#1

ME & YOU FAVORITES

THING TO DO ON A LAZY DAY

NICKNAME I CALL YOU

GIFT I'VE GIVEN YOU

MOVIE WE'VE WATCHED

PHOTO OF US

ADVENTURE WE'VE BEEN ON

COMPLIMENT I'VE GIVEN YOU

WHAT ARE THE LOVE LANGUAGES?

WORDS OF AFFIRMATION
Expressing love through verbal encouragement, compliments, and kind words.

RECEIVING GIFTS
Demonstrating love with meaningful, thoughtful presents that reflect care and attention.

QUALITY TIME
Undivided attention and shared activities to build connection and intimacy.

ACTS OF SERVICE
Showing love by doing helpful or thoughtful things, like chores or errands, to ease your partner's burden.

PHYSICAL TOUCH
Communicating love through physical affection, like hugs, kisses, or holding hands.

LOVE LANGUAGE QUIZ

How do you like to celebrate your birthday?
A. Hearing heartfelt toasts and messages
B. Opening lots of presents and receiving thoughtful gifts
C. A day filled with special activities planned by my partner
D. Having my partner take care of all the details so I can relax
E. Being showered with hugs and kisses all day

What makes you feel closest to your partner?
A. When they tell me how much they love and value me
B. When they spontaneously give me a thoughtful present
C. When they plan a date just for the two of us
D. When they go out of their way to help me with things
E. When they hold my hand or give me a back rub

Which of these would mean the most to you on a rough day?
A. My partner saying, "I'm here for you"
B. A surprise treat like my favorite snack
C. My partner making time to sit and listen to me
D. My partner doing the dishes or chores without being asked
E. A comforting hug or cuddle on the couch

What's the best way for your partner to show they're thinking of you?
A. Sending a sweet text or leaving a note
B. Bringing home a small, meaningful gift
C. Arranging a special date or outing
D. Offering to take something off my plate
E. Giving me a spontaneous hug or kiss

#1

LOVE LANGUAGE QUIZ

How do you like to celebrate your birthday?

A. Hearing heartfelt toasts and messages
B. Receiving thoughtful gifts
C. A day filled with special activities planned by my partner
D. Having my partner take care of all the details so I can relax
E. Being showered with hugs and kisses all day

What makes you feel closest to your partner?

A. When they tell me how much they love and value me
B. When they spontaneously give me a thoughtful present
C. When they plan a date just for the two of us
D. When they go out of their way to help me with things
E. When they hold my hand or give me a back rub

Which of these would mean the most to you on a rough day?

A. My partner saying, "I'm here for you"
B. A surprise treat like my favorite snack
C. My partner making time to sit and listen to me
D. My partner doing the dishes or chores without being asked
E. A comforting hug or cuddle on the couch

What's the best way for your partner to show they're thinking of you?

A. Sending a sweet text or leaving a note
B. Bringing home a small, meaningful gift
C. Arranging a special date or outing
D. Offering to take something off my plate
E. Giving me a spontaneous hug or kiss

#2

LOVE LANGUAGE QUIZ Results

If you answered with...

mostly A's, your love language is
WORDS OF AFFIRMATION

mostly B's, your love language is
RECEIVING GIFTS

mostly C's, your love language is
QUALITY TIME

mostly D's, your love language is
ACTS OF SERVICE

mostly E's, your love language is
PHYSICAL TOUCH

WHAT IS YOUR FAVORITE

show, movie, or podcast we watch together?

#1

WHAT IS YOUR FAVORITE

show, movie, or podcast we watch together?

#2

HOW
I SEE YOU

MY FAVORITE
QUALITY OF YOURS:

YOU MAKE ME
SMILE WHEN:

IF YOU WERE
AN ANIMAL,
YOU WOULD BE:

IF YOU WERE
A COLOR,
YOU WOULD BE:

SOMETHING YOU
DO BETTER THAN
ANYONE ELSE:

ONE THING YOU
DO THAT MAKES
ME PROUD:

SOMETHING SMALL
YOU DO THAT
I APPRECIATE:

ONE THING
I ADMIRE
ABOUT YOU:

HOW I SEE YOU

#2

MY FAVORITE
QUALITY OF YOURS:

YOU MAKE ME
SMILE WHEN:

IF YOU WERE
AN ANIMAL,
YOU WOULD BE:

IF YOU WERE
A COLOR,
YOU WOULD BE:

SOMETHING YOU
DO BETTER THAN
ANYONE ELSE:

ONE THING YOU
DO THAT MAKES
ME PROUD:

SOMETHING SMALL
YOU DO THAT
I APPRECIATE:

ONE THING
I ADMIRE
ABOUT YOU:

REASONS WHY
• I LOVE YOU •

#2